Fingerpower®
Level One

Technic for All Piano Methods

by John W. Schaum

Edited by Wesley Schaum

FOREWORD

Strong fingers are an important requirement for all pianists, amateur and professional. Schaum Fingerpower® exercises are designed to strengthen all five fingers of both hands.

Equal hand development is assured by the performance of the same patterns in each hand. The exercises are short and easily memorized. This enables the student to focus his/her efforts on technical benefits, listening attentively, and playing with a steady beat.

A measure number (enclosed in a small box) is included at the beginning of each system of music. This makes it easier to locate measures during the lesson and for written practice assignments.

The exercises become progressively more difficult as the student moves through the book. This makes the exercises an ideal companion to a method book at the same level.

The series consists of seven books, Primer Level through Level 6.

To access audio, visit:
www.halleonard.com/mylibrary

7987-5006-3923-3051

ISBN 978-1-936098-92-7

EXCLUSIVELY DISTRIBUTED BY

HAL•LEONARD®

Visit Hal Leonard Online at
www.halleonard.com

Contact Us:
Hal Leonard
7777 West Bluemound Road
Milwaukee, WI 53213
Email: info@halleonard.com

In Europe contact:
Hal Leonard Europe Limited
Distribution Centre, Newmarket Road
Bury St Edmunds, Suffolk, IP33 3YB
Email: info@halleonardeurope.com

In Australia contact:
Hal Leonard Australia Pty. Ltd.
4 Lentara Court
Cheltenham, Victoria, 3192 Australia
Email: info@halleonard.com.au

CONTENTS

PRACTICE SUGGESTIONS

To derive the full benefit from these exercises, they should be played with a firm, solid finger action. **Listen carefully while practicing**. Try to play **each finger equally loud**. Each hand should also play equally loud. It is also important to be aware of the feeling in your fingers and hands during practice.

Each exercise should be practiced four or five times daily, starting at a slow tempo and gradually increasing the tempo as proficiency improves. Several previously learned exercises should be reviewed each week as part of regular practice.

ABOUT THE AUDIO

To access the accompanying audio, go to **www.halleonard.com/mylibrary** and enter the code found on the first page of this book. This will grant you instant access to every example.

There are two tracks for each exercise:
1. Slow practice tempo
2. Performance tempo

The solo part is emphasized on the practice track. The accompaniment is emphasized on the performance track. There are two extra count-in measures before each track.

Follow these three steps for practice variety. At first, the steps should be done with the slow practice tempo. The same steps may be used again at the performance tempo.

1. Student plays right hand only
2. Student plays left hand only
3. Student plays both hands together

1. Two-Finger Phrase (2/4)

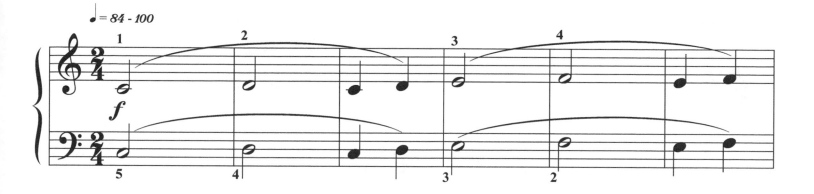

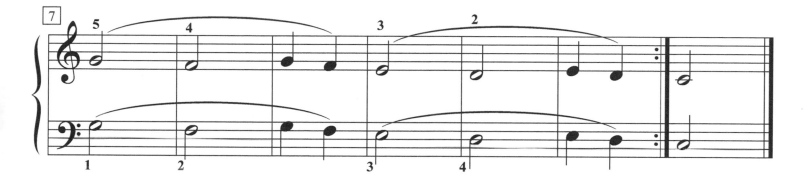

2. Two-Finger Phrase (3/4)

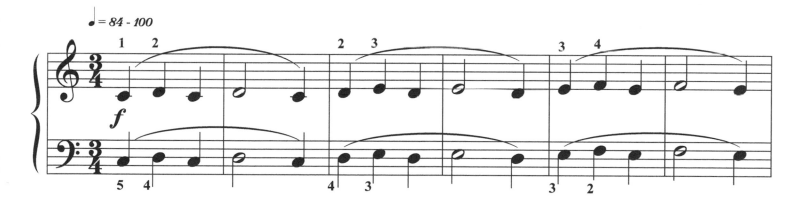

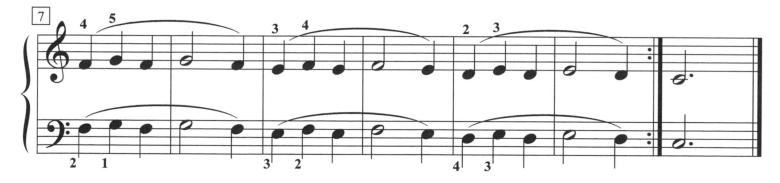

3. Two-Finger Phrase (4/4)

4. Three-Finger Phrase (2/4)

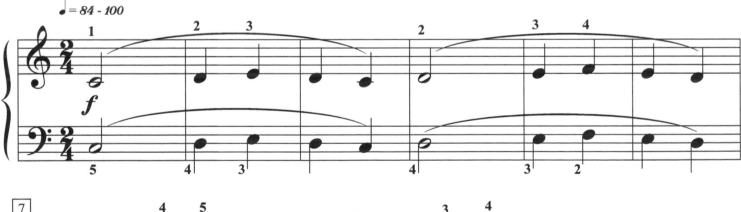

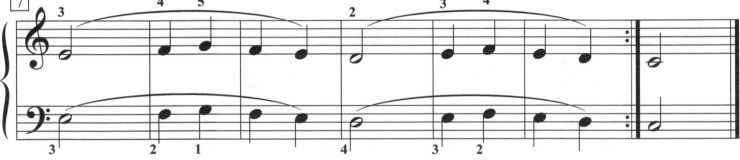

Teacher's Note: Cross-hand work is excellent for developing **independence of the hands.** For extra work, have the student play Exercise No. 4 crossing the Right hand OVER the Left hand. Right hand plays the notes in the **Bass** staff. Left hand plays notes in the **Treble** staff. Many other exercises in this book may also be played in cross-hand style.

5. Three-Finger Phrase (3/4)

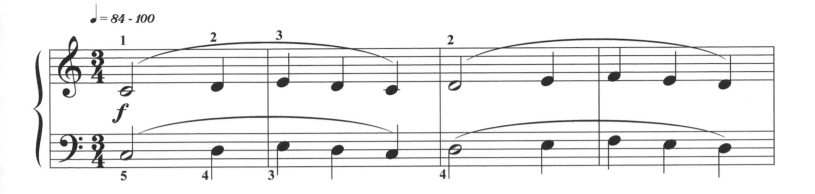

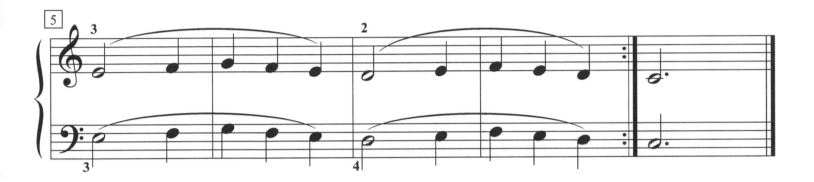

6. Three-Finger Phrase (4/4)

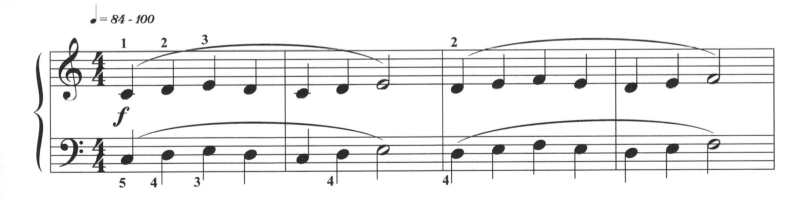

7. Four-Finger Phrase (2/4)

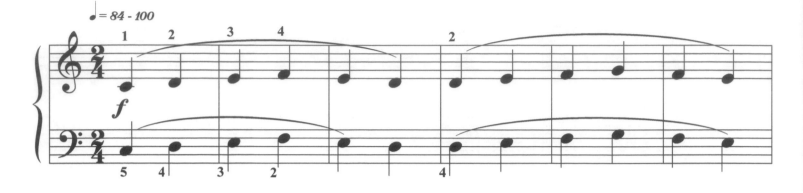

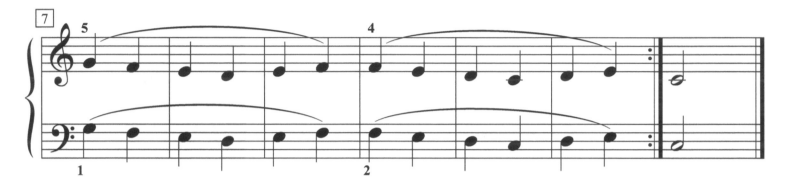

8. Four-Finger Phrase (3/4)

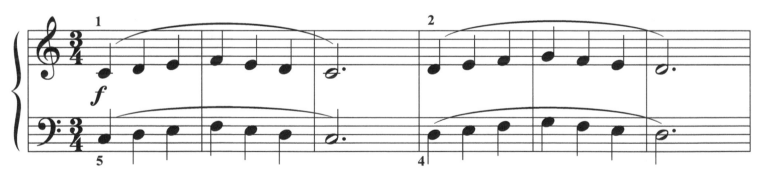

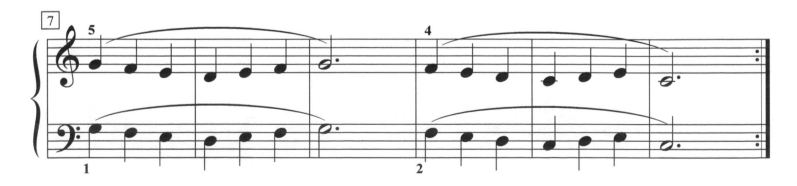

9. Four-Finger Phrase (4/4)

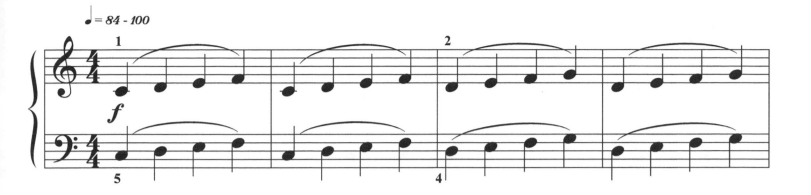

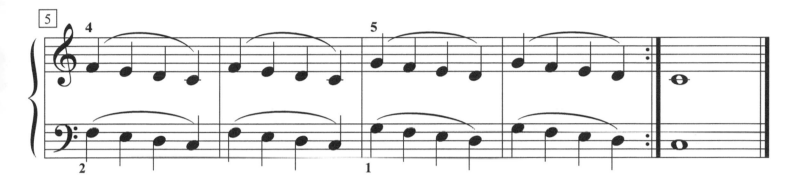

10. Five-Finger Acceleration Study

11. Five-Finger Phrase (2/4)

12. Five-Finger Phrase (3/4)

13. Etude for Five Fingers

Note: An etude *(AY-tood)* is a musical study. Also practice the above etude in the following rhythm pattern:

14. Legato and Staccato

15. Legato and Staccato

(Combined)

Teacher's Note: Previous exercises may be reviewed by playing one hand staccato and the other hand legato.

16. Staccato Study

(Alternating Left and Right)

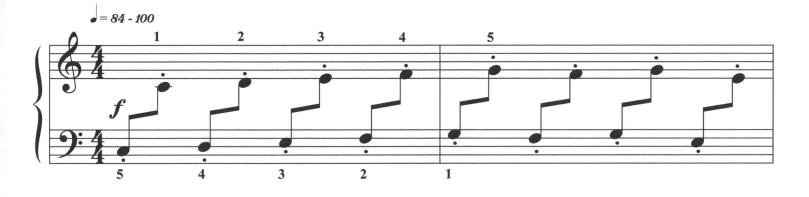

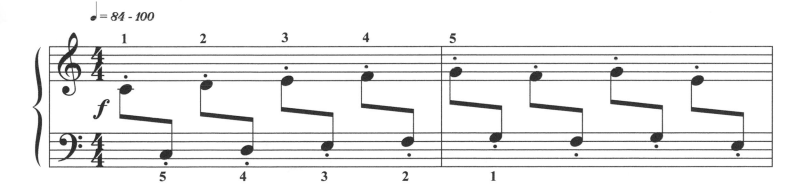

17. Staccato Study

(Alternating Right and Left)

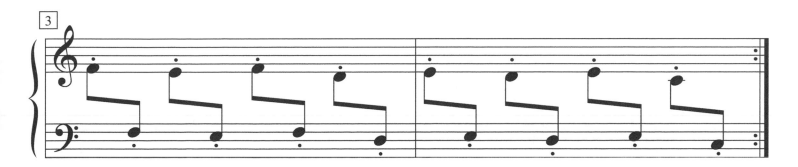

18. Intervals of a Third (2/4)

19. Intervals of a Third (3/4)

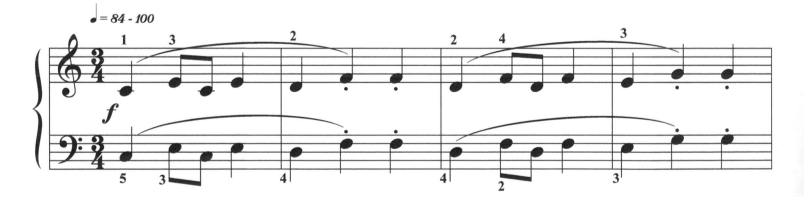

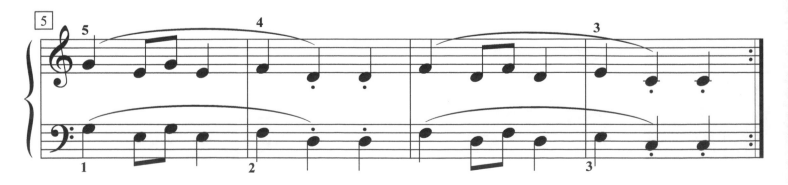

20. Etude in Broken Thirds

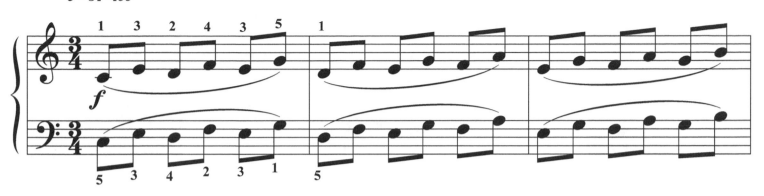

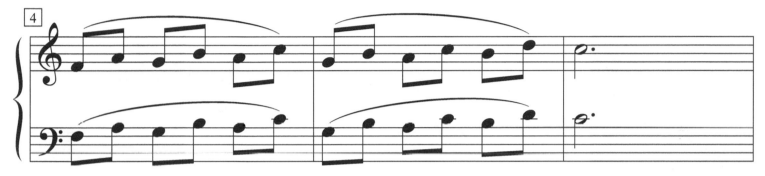

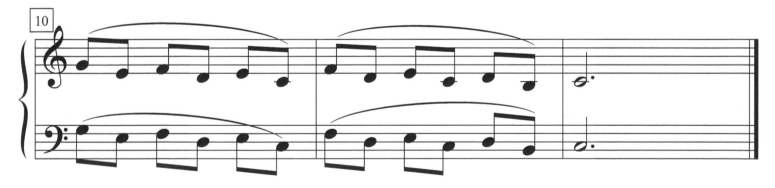

Special Assignment: Practice each hand separately in blocked thirds:

21. Etude in Broken Fourths

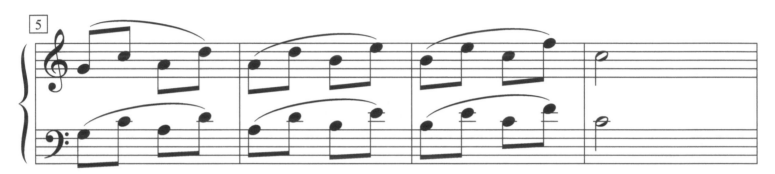

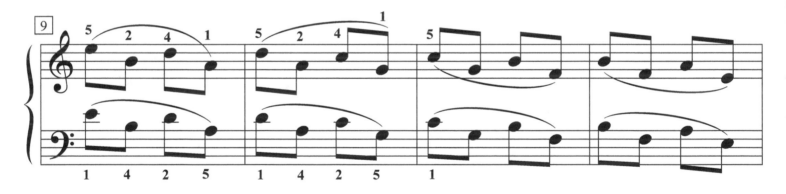

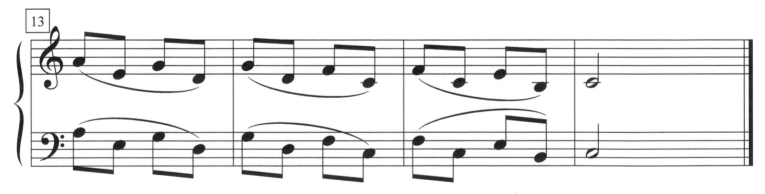

Special Assignment: Practice each hand separately in blocked fourths:

22. Etude in Broken Fifths

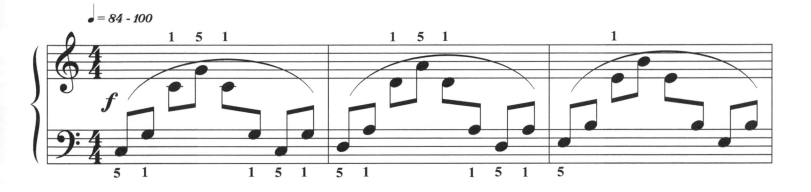

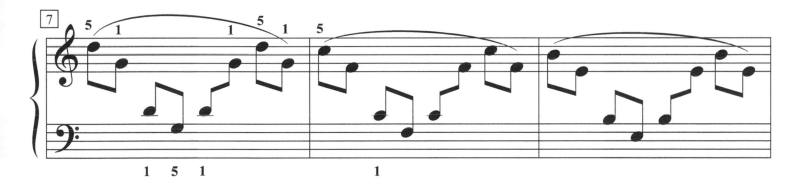

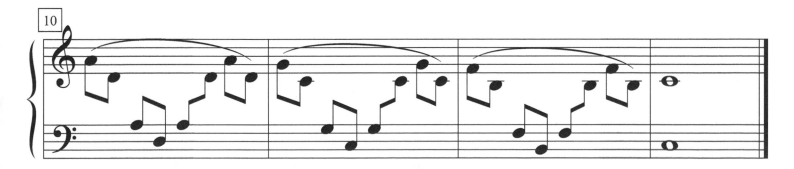

Special Assignment: Practice in blocked fifths as follows:

etc.

23. Etude in Thirds

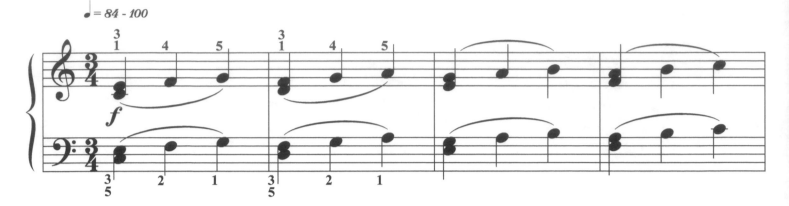

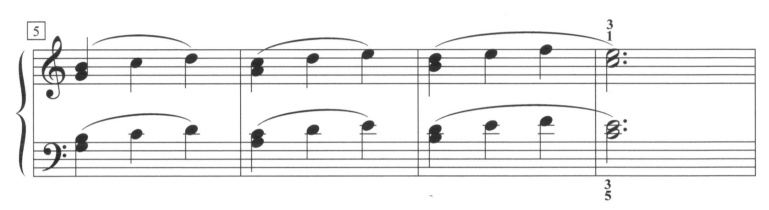

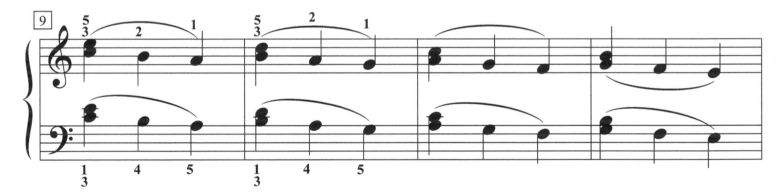

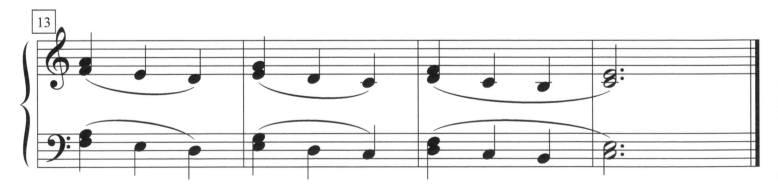

24. Finger Extension Etude

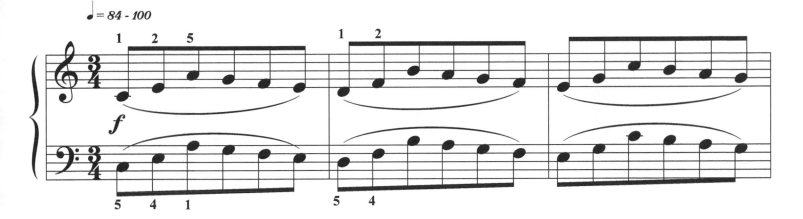

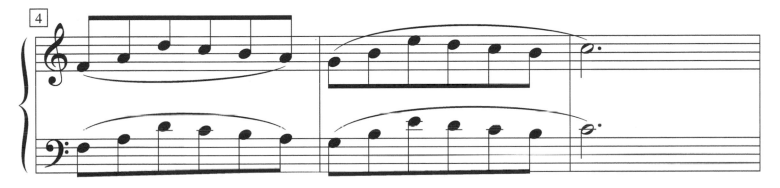

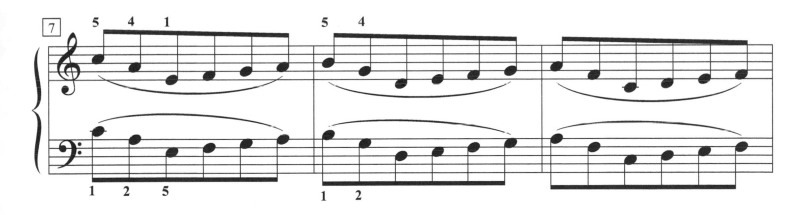

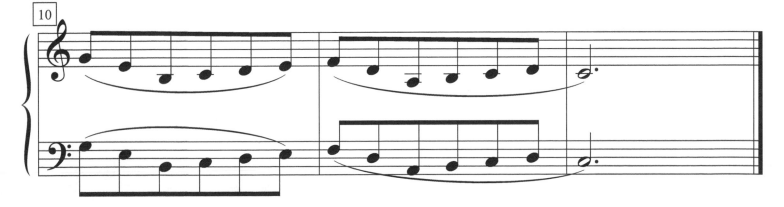

25. Triads

(Broken and Blocked)

Special Assignment: The five studies on pages 18 through 23 are all built on the triads in the key of C major. It is recommended that these five studies be transposed to other major keys. This can be done by examining the triads of the examples below.

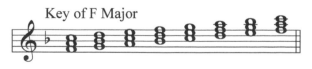

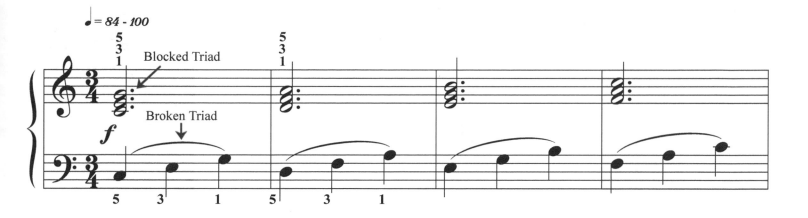

26. Triads

(Blocked and Broken)

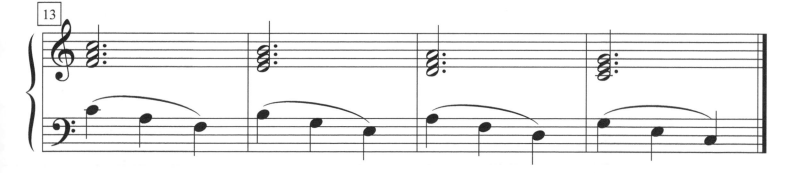

27. Arpeggio Etude

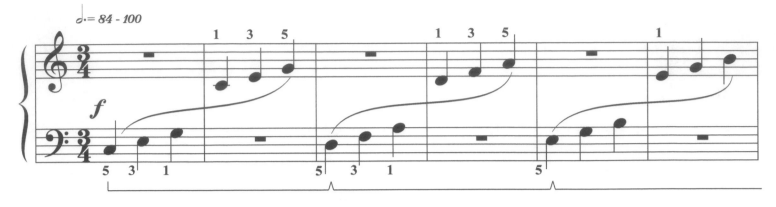

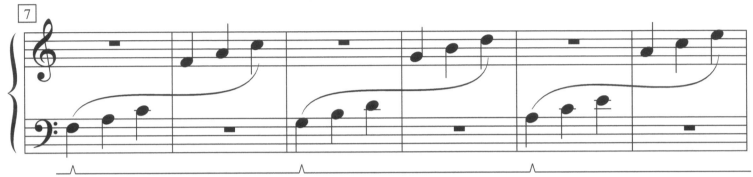

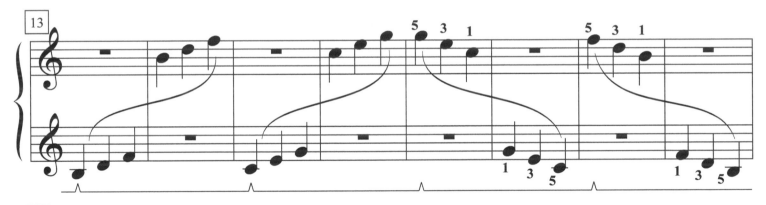

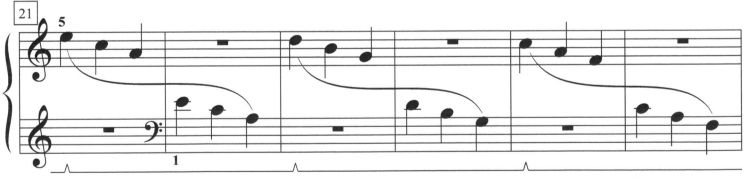

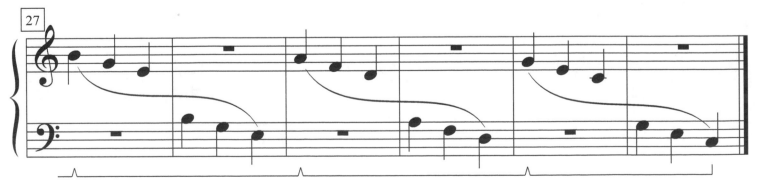

28. Massive Triad Etude

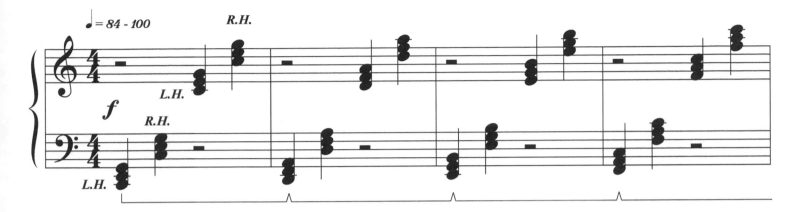

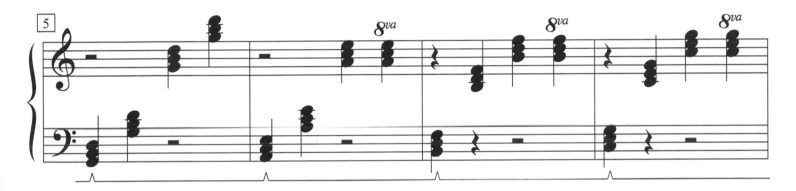

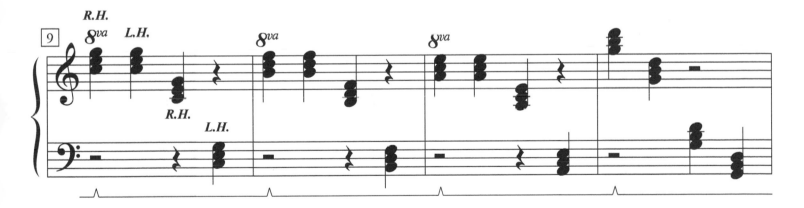

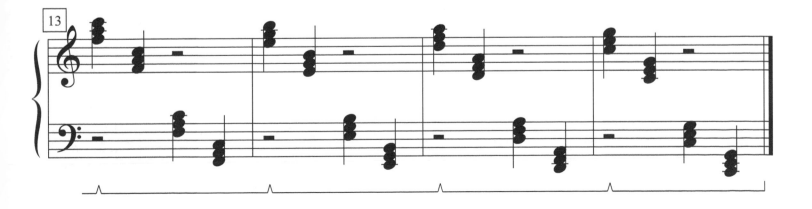

29. Grand Arpeggio Etude

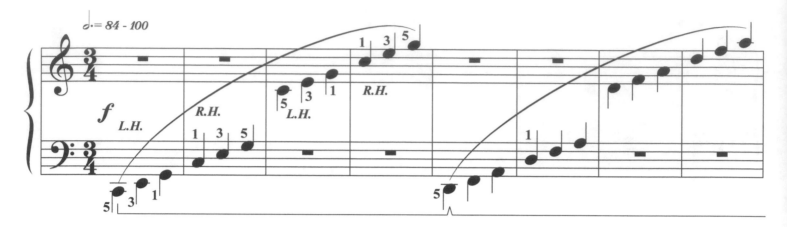

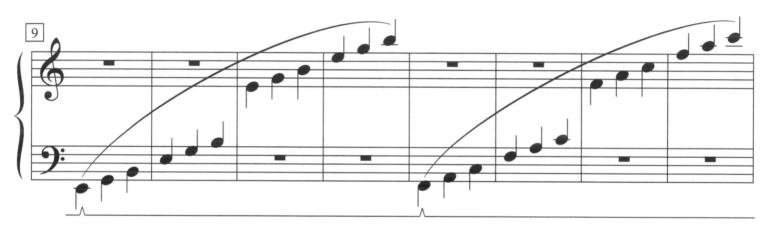

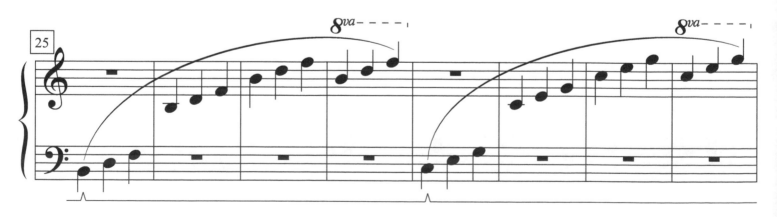

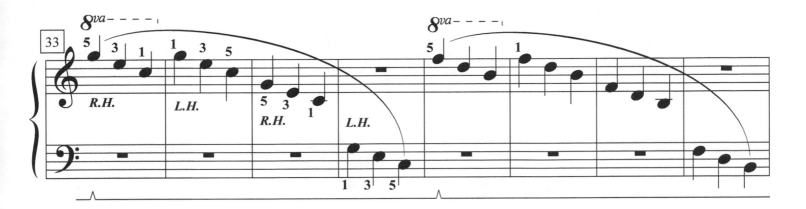

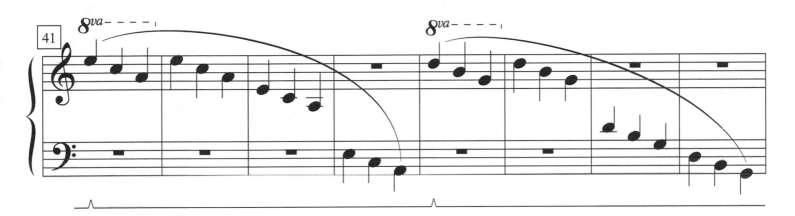

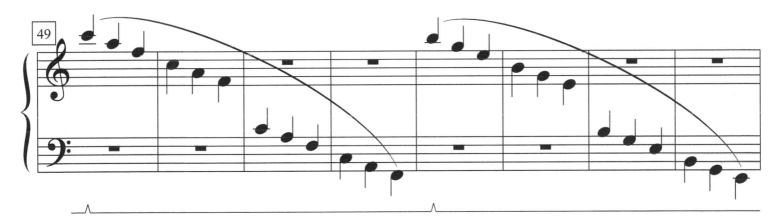

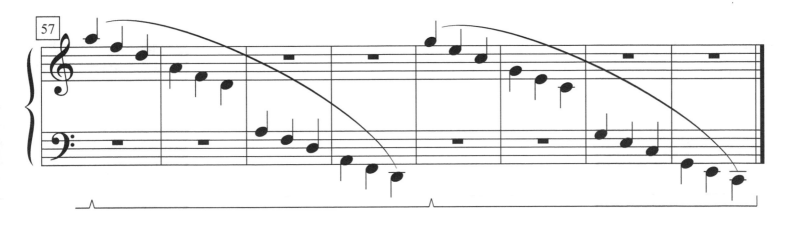

You are now ready to progress to Schaum FINGERPOWER®, Level Two.

MORE GREAT SCHAUM PUBLICATIONS

FINGERPOWER®
by John W. Schaum
Physical training and discipline are needed for both athletics and keyboard playing. Keyboard muscle conditioning is called technique. technique exercises are as important to the keyboard player as workouts and calisthenics are to the athlete. Schaum's *Fingerpower®* books are dedicated to development of individual finger strength and dexterity in both hands.

00645334	Primer Level – Book Only	$7.99
00645016	Primer Level – Book/Audio	$9.99
00645335	Level 1 – Book Only	$6.99
00645019	Level 1 – Book/Audio	$8.99
00645336	Level 2 – Book Only	$7.99
00645022	Level 2 – Book/Audio	$9.99
00645337	Level 3 – Book Only	$6.99
00645025	Level 3 – Book/Audio	$7.99
00645338	Level 4 – Book Only	$6.99
00645028	Level 4 – Book/Audio	$9.99
00645339	Level 5 Book Only	$7.99
00645340	Level 6 Book Only	$7.99

FINGERPOWER® ETUDES
Melodic exercises crafted by master technique composers. Modified or transposed etudes provide equal hand development with a planned variety of technical styles, keys, and time signatures.

00645392	Primer Level	$6.99
00645393	Level 1	$6.99
00645394	Level 2	$6.99
00645395	Level 3	$6.99
00645396	Level 4	$6.99

FINGERPOWER® FUN
arr. Wesley Schaum
Early Elementary Level
Musical experiences beyond the traditional *Fingerpower®* books that include fun-to-play pieces with finger exercises and duet accompaniments. Short technique preparatory drills (finger workouts) focus on melodic patterns found in each piece.

00645126	Primer Level	$6.95
00645127	Level 1	$6.99
00645128	Level 2	$6.95
00645129	Level 3	$6.99
00645144	Level 4	$6.95

FINGERPOWER® POP
arr. by James Poteat
10 great pop piano solo arrangements with fun technical warm-ups that complement the *Fingerpower®* series! Can also be used as motivating supplements to any method and in any learning situation.

00237508	Primer Level	$9.99
00237510	Level 1	$9.99
00282865	Level 2	$9.99
00282866	Level 3	$9.99
00282867	Level 4	$10.99

FINGERPOWER® TRANSPOSER
by Wesley Schaum
Early Elementary Level
This book includes 21 short, 8-measure exercises using 5-finger patterns. Positions are based on C,F, and G major and no key signatures are used. Patterns involve intervals of 3rds, 4ths, and 5ths up and down and are transposed from C to F and F to C, C to G and G to C, G to F and F to G.

00645150	Primer Level	$6.95
00645151	Level 1	$6.95
00645152	Level 2	$6.95
00645154	Level 3	$6.95
00645156	Level 4	$6.99

JUMBO STAFF MANUSCRIPT BOOK
This pad features 24 pages with 4 staves per page.
00645936 . . . . $4.25

CERTIFICATE OF MUSICAL ACHIEVEMENT
Reward your students for their hard work with these official 8x10-inch certificates that you can customize. 12 per package.
00645938 . . . . $6.99

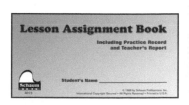

SCHAUM LESSON ASSIGNMENT BOOK
by John Schaum
With space for 32 weeks, this book will help keep students on the right track for their practice time.
00645935 . . . . $3.95

HAL•LEONARD®
www.halleonard.com

0322

Prices, contents, and availability subject to change without notice.

355

Schaum Fingerpower®

Effective Technic for Students of All Ages

Short, progressive exercises

Designed to strengthen all fingers of both hands

Supplements all piano and keyboard methods

Audio accompaniments available for Primer through Level 4

Primer - Level 6

Fingerpower® Etudes

Melodic exercises by master technic composers are fun to practice

Practical and pleasing variety of technic styles in each book

Primer - Level 4

Fingerpower® FUN

Fun to play melodies with many technic benefits

Short technic preparatory drill focuses on melodic patterns found in each piece

Planned variety of rhythms, key signatures, time signatures, dynamics and use of staccato

Primer - Level 4

The price of this book includes access to audio tracks online, for download or streaming, using the unique code inside the book.

Now including **PLAYBACK+,** a multi-functional audio player that allows you to slow down audio without changing pitch, set loop points, change keys, and pan left or right—available exclusively from Hal Leonard.

U.S. $9.99

08148 30421 9

HL00645019

Schaum

EXCLUSIVELY DISTRIBUTED BY

HAL•LEONARD®

ISBN 978-1-936098-92-7

9 781936 098927